30 DAYS TO GETTING ORGANIZED

By Gary Holland

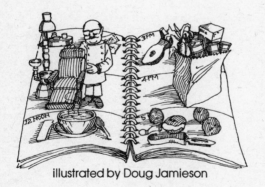

illustrated by Doug Jamieson

A BANTAM BOOK

TORONTO · NEW YORK · LONDON · SYDNEY

30 DAYS TO GETTING ORGANIZED
A Bantam Book / February 1984

Produced by Cloverdale Press
133 Fifth Avenue
New York, New York 10003

ISBN 0-553-34048-4

Published simultaneously in the United States and Canada

Bantam Books are published by Bantam Books, Inc. Its trademark, consisting of the
words "Bantam Books" and the portrayal of a rooster, is Registered in U.S. Patent
and Trademark Office and in other countries. Marca Registrada. Bantam Books,
Inc., 666 Fifth Avenue, New York, New York 10103.

PRINTED IN THE UNITED STATES OF AMERICA

CW   0   9   8   7   6   5   4   3   2   1

CONTENTS

Things fall apart; the centre cannot hold . . .
—W. B. Yeats

It ain't necessarily so.
—Sportin' Life
Porgy and Bess

Not Really an Introduction

So Read It!

Getting organized in 30 days seems like a lofty goal to those of us who have spent a lifetime becoming disorganized—when the hall closet has taken years to get into that shape!

If you have spent years missing appointments, putting things off, living in disarray and missing out on a lot of fun because you have to spend so much time and energy maintaining what little order you do have, notice this: A lot of people are on time. They get things done. Their homes are neat. Their closets even are organized. Once on the critical list myself when it came to organization, I began to wonder how this could be. I began to observe these wonders and ask them questions. And eventually I set out on what earlier would have been considered a nigh impossible task— getting organized.

Organization *is* possible. Chaos doesn't rule the universe. As a matter of fact, neatness and pattern may be the very nature of things.

Before you go put all the spoons together in the silverware drawer, let me add this:

Your life will not be running like clockwork in 30 days. Your home will not be ready for *Better Homes and Gardens*. You will not be elected the most organized person of the year.

Rather, in 30 days you will have th
framework, the methodology, for getting your li
in order. Do not become too soon discouraged if i
30 days your basement is still a mess. What yo
hope to achieve is a handle on how and when yo
want to get around to it. When you take control o
your life, a packed closet will not keep the rest o
your life from being orderly.

Every system for getting organized has to b
personal, flexible and realistic. Turn this into
60-day course if you wish. Modify sections to su
yourself. Or ignore whole sections altogether.

So get ready to defy your nature and ge
organized!

1

WEEK ONE: ORGANIZING TIME

Way back in high school science, we all learned that, according to the Second Law of Thermodynamics, it is the very nature of things to fall into disorder. We will disprove this scientific finding by tackling Time the first week. In the next chapter, we will handle Space.

DAY 1, HOUR 1: MAKE A LIST

Enough talk. It's time to act.

Get a piece of paper—any piece will do for now—and make the following list of things to purchase:

datebook

small notebook

memo pad

colored pens

Do not rush right out and buy these things. The first lesson of getting organized is: Don't be impulsive or compulsive. Getting organized means proceeding about your business in a rational, thoughtful manner.

> *Example*: Suppose you had made out this list, hopped in your car, gone to the stationery store, bought the things and come home. A few hours later, you might have discovered you needed milk—back in the car to the grocery store. Then you might have remembered you had clothes at the cleaner. You'd be surprised just how many people act so haphazardly.

The Importance of Lists

This book could have been called *Another The Book of Lists* because we're going to make a lot of them.

You have just made one, and, small as it is, it is still important. (Hold onto it for a while, we're not ready to act on it just yet.)

Lists provide important services:

• *Lists get information out of your head and onto a piece of paper.* In other words, you can now stop thinking about that item; it's not cluttering up your brain. (The other choice if you have to get something done is not to write it down. This requires you to rush right out and do it lest you forget. And that is a random rather than an organized course of action.)

• *Lists actually help you remember things.* If you have written "soap" then forget your list when you go to the grocery store, the very process of writing the item down will help you remember to buy soap anyway.

Making a list commits you to an action and burns that commitment into your brain while at the same time getting it out of your conscious thoughts.

• *Lists help you consolidate and organize things and actions.* More about this in a minute.

• *Things on a list can be crossed off.* There is a subtle psychological reward in accomplishing something and crossing it off your list. We are interested in rewards because, especially during the first weeks of your organizing, it will be easy to "fall off the wagon." Rewards will reinforce your determination to get and stay organized.

Break down chores so that you can reward yourself more often. Instead of "clean the house," break down this chore into rooms or even smaller tasks. Instead of "go to the stationery store," compile, as we did, a list comprised of the different things you need to buy. Cross off each item as you do or acquire it.

Routing Yourself

Back to our list.

Add some things you need to do or purchase. Perhaps the list now looks something like this:

datebook

small notebook

memo pad

different colored pens

dry cleaner

milk

eggs

pick up Johnny

vegetable for dinner

Now we have a list we can work with. There are three steps involved.

• *Consolidate it.* The first four items can be picked up in the stationery store, and they are already grouped together. Milk, eggs and vegetable are all grocery-store items. The dry cleaner and picking up Johnny are unrelated individual items. You have nine things to get or do, four stops to make.

• *Consider time.* Johnny needs to be gotten at 3:30. Write this down.

• *Route yourself.* Budgeting your time appropriately and being geographically sensible, route yourself in as neat a little circle as possible, with no avoidable backtracking or criss-crossing. Code your list like this:

1 *datebook*

1 *small notebook*

1 *memo pad*

1 *different colored pens*

4 *dry cleaner*

2 *milk*

2 *eggs*

3 *pick up Johnny*

2 *vegetable for dinner*

The first stop to make when you leave home is the stationery store; second, the grocery store; third, Johnny and fourth, the dry cleaner.

If it doesn't seem like routing your activities could be all that helpful, consider this: How many times have you needed to accomplish only one thing, such as going to the bank, yet walk right past it on your way to your office, necessitating a special trip later? As our lives become more and more complicated, routing oneself becomes more and more necessary.

The Supplies

The items on the first list are the tools to getting organized.

• *A combination datebook/calendar*. Get whatever kind you are going to feel comfortable using. But here are a few things you might like to consider:

The *monthly calendar* (with pretty pictures—or pretty bodies) that hangs on the wall is probably too general, the boxes too small to fit much information, but if you think it will work for you, try it. (You can always get a better one later.)

The *daily calendar* (the typical office fare) doesn't give enough of an overview of your week to be very helpful, though there is plenty of room for each day's activities.

The *week-at-a-glance calendar* comes in many different styles and forms, but they all show you "at a glance" how your week is shaping up—and with a quick flip of the page how the next week looks, too. One style breaks down the day by half hours, which is helpful for organizing business appointments. You may not need anything quite so detailed. Do make sure, however, that there is room for writing down things that are not keyed into a set time.

No matter which type of organizational calendar you choose, buy one that looks great (maybe even an elegant leather-bound one), one that you won't mind leaving out on your desk or end table. When you purchase something really nice, it's a pleasure to use it. And that will encourage you to use it. (But whatever you do, don't buy one that's so nice you don't want to use it at all.)

• *A small spiral notebook*. Get one that is very compact, that you can carry in your purse, briefcase or even pocket. This is to write things down on—anything as a matter of fact, whether it pertains to helping you stay organized or not—when your other memo pad (see below) or calendar is not handy. Most writers carry small pads like this with them everywhere to jot down thoughts whenever they occur.

• *A memo pad*. There isn't really much difference between the notebook and the memo pad. Keep the memo pad at home—by the phone to jot things down on while talking to people or working, or attached to the refrigerator to record needed supplies. Later we'll discuss more fully how to use these items. For now you might want to purchase two memo pads.

• *Colored pens*. You probably already have plenty of pens, and some colored pens, too. Sometimes when you have new, fresh tools to work with, as with the calendar, it's more fun to work. Buy three colors of pens. (You can buy any colors. Here we will be using red, blue and green. We'll learn what the colors stand for later.)

THE REST OF WEEK 1

We will not break down the rest of Week One's activities on a day-by-day basis. That would be imposing an arbitrary and artificial structure on your time when you may find you want to proceed more slowly or (a bit) more quickly.

However, the first unit of time—whether it be a week, five days or ten days—should be spent on organizing *time*. Once you organize your time more carefully, you should discover more time that can be spent organizing other aspects of your life.

Using the Notebook

You will use your notebook for miscellaneous items and errands that occur to you during the day. For example, your memo pad is at home (on the desk, attached to the refrigerator), and on the way to work you notice the circus is in town. Wouldn't it be nice to get tickets? You also step in a puddle and notice that your black shoes have a hole in them. So in your little notebook you write, "circus tickets" and "get shoes half-soled." If you can't write these things down right away, do it as soon as possible.

You perhaps can use this notebook to good advantage for other things, too. Since ideally you have it with you at all times, you can use it to write down thoughts and ideas that occur to you during the day, maybe a stock price or an idea for a Christmas party. Just flip the notebook over and use the pages starting from the back so that these thoughts don't get confused with the other items you list in the front.

Using the Memo Pad

The memo pad, at home, is that thing on which you

will write down everything you will need to buy and do—the soap for tomorrow's shower, the errands you need to run this afternoon.

Keep the pad in a convenient spot so you can jot things down as they occur to you or as you notice that you need them. (If you have a large family so that your grocery list alone rivals *War and Peace*, you may want to keep a separate list for food. If picking up Johnny gets lost between lettuce, toothpaste, corn flakes and window cleaner, Johnny may get left, which we must avoid. In this case as well, keep your grocery or supply list and your errand list separate.)

Beginning to Use the Datebook

While the memo pad and notebook are key items that organize things and route yourself, they are still fairly simple tools. The datebook is just as basic but much more complex, and we will refine its use throughout this book, returning to it often. There's a logical approach to using a datebook.

• *Establish how your datebook is organized.* Knowing how it works will help you use it better.

• *Write down in blue ink any continuing obligations.* For example: If you take dance lessons every Thursday at 2:00 P.M., block out every Thursday at 2:00 P.M. for at least a month or so, or as long as the lessons will continue. If there's something you do every day at the same time— like picking up Johnny—you may want just to draw a line through that time slot. (You will know what it means.)

• *Add upcoming appointments*. These include any other things that are on your agenda in the weeks to come—dinner parties, doctor's appointments, theater dates, and so forth. Use blue ink for things that are definite, pencil for things that might change. Use red ink for something that is urgent or crucial (this applies to your memo pad, too; red indicates something that *must* be done or acquired). Flag or underline in red something written in blue ink that takes on an urgency.

• *Note every new date or appointment*. If your clothes will be ready at the dry cleaner on Friday and you need them for the weekend, write "dry cleaner" in pencil somewhere in the Friday space. When Friday comes, you can plan more precisely when to pick up your clothes.

NOTE: You can use any color scheme you choose. But remember, the categories are Definite (blue), Urgent (red), Previously cancelled (green), Indefinite (pencil).

Organizing a Day

Once a day, ideally over morning coffee, you should sit down and look at your lists and your datebook, and plan your day. (At this time, also try to think of things that need to be done and add them to your lists.) You can organize your day one of two ways, whichever works best for you. Here's the first way:

If your day appears filled with many appointments, and your memo pad and notebook have fewer items, you may want to route your day in your datebook. For example, your day and your list may look like this:

Datebook	
9:30	Dentist appointment
12:00	Lunch with Mom
2:00	Dance lesson
3:30	Pick up Johnny
4:30	Take Johnny to tuba lesson
8:00	Watch TV special

Memo/Notebook
Circus tickets
Get shoes half-soled
Check to tuba teacher
Milk
Eggs
Dry Cleaner
Write letter to Aunt Grace

Now think about the day—how much time will your different appointments take? where are they in relation to one another?—and devise a route for your day, something that looks like this perhaps:

9:00	*Shoes to shoemaker*	(Because it's on the way to the dentist.)
9:30	*Dentist appointment*	(Better leave the time slot after this open because you never know how much time it will take.)
12:00	*Lunch with Mom*	
2:00	*Dance lesson*	
3:15	*Dry cleaner*	
3:30	*Pick up Johnny*	
4:00	*Buying groceries*	(This may not be the most convenient route geographically, but it works out best time-wise. You can drag Johnny with you, and then drop him off at the tuba lesson afterwards without having to go home in between.)
4:30	*Take Johnny to tuba lesson*	

```
8:00 Watch TV special    (This may be pen-
                         ciled in your book
                         because it isn't
                         something you have
                         to do, but if the day
                         goes well and there
                         is time, you will do
                         it. It's nice to make
                         "leisure time" ap-
                         pointments with
                         yourself like this.)
```

You probably have noticed that everything on the memo list hasn't been taken care of. After you've moved certain items into your datebook, the list should look something like this:

Circus tickets

Milk

Eggs

Write letter to Aunt Grace

Items #2 and #6 have been crossed off because you have moved them to the datebook list. Items #4 and #5 have been underlined in red ink because you need them for dinner. Item #3 is crossed off because you paperclip the check for the tuba teacher to the datebook (ideally you had the check previously written when you paid all of your other monthly bills—more of this in Chapter 3).

Now you take this messy looking list and attach it
to the datebook, too, so that when you get to the
grocery store you have your grocery list with you.
(Cross milk and eggs off after you've bought
them.) It also reminds you that should you find
some time during the day, you could swing by the
circus to get tickets or write to Aunt Grace.

Now let's consider if unforeseen things happen during the day.

What If	Then You
You get to the shoe-maker, and the shop is closed.	*Reschedule this errand.* (You don't need to make another note to get your shoes fixed; it's already in your datebook for the next time you sit down to make plans.)
Your dentist appointment left you in such pain that you had to re-schedule lunch with Mom.	*Record the new date in green ink—or flag it with green ink later when you have a colored pen handy.* (Green means you have postponed, cancelled, or not accom-plished something. It may be important for you, socially or in busi-ness, to know how many times you've broken a particular appointment. If an engagement gets

postponed again, put a little green *2* by the notation. In a sense, this is a way of making yourself aware of what things you may be avoiding!

The dentist must see you tomorrow afternoon at 3:00 (the only time available) to complete the agony he began today.	*Record the dentist appointment for 3:00 tomorrow in red ink.* (Make a note to make other arrangements to pick up Johnny at school.)
You didn't get the circus tickets or write to Aunt Grace.	*Write down "circus tickets" and "letter to Aunt Grace"* in green ink on a new memo list. (If the circus won't be in town much longer, you might use red ink for that entry.)

Now you can throw away your memo list. Everything on it has either been done or transferred. Remember to cross off everything on your calendar that you accomplished (even the TV show). This gives you a visual reminder of those things that you haven't accomplished. Anything without a line through it jumps right off the page, and you can reschedule it for a new time.

Method #2 should be used if your memo and notebook lists are long and you have only a few datebook entries.

Instead of transferring the list from you
memo book into your datebook, transfer your ap
pointments to your memo list. Then consolidat
the lists and route yourself accordingly, the wa
we did it at the very beginning of this chapter.

Either method works. With method #1, yo
carry your datebook around with you; method #
has you carrying your memo list. With eithe
method, make sure you cross off completed item
and transfer items not completed.

Organizing Long-Term Items

Using only this day-by-day plan could drive yo
mad, as your lists grow and you have to star
transferring hundreds of items from one day to th
next.

There are things of low priority that shouldn'
get on a day-by-day list or schedule. Our goal i
method not madness. Such low-priority items ca
be considered long-term items.

For instance, using some of our old examples
If Aunt Grace has written you a letter saying sh
would like to give Johnny a pet raccoon for hi
birthday (they just found a baby one on thei
farm), you might want to write "letter to Aun
Grace" in red ink, complete with exclamatio
points, on your memo pad. It's a priority—mus
do—chore (unless you're fond of raccoons).

On the other hand, if Aunt Grace has writte
asking Johnny to come stay for a week, unles
you're very anxious to get rid of him, we'll handl
it another way.

In your week-at-a-glance datebook, ther

should be an extra column for notes. Here write down such things as:

Write to Aunt Grace

Duplicate keys for summer house

Get circus tickets

Buy new Streisand album

Clean oven

These are things to be done during the course of the week whenever time allows. Maybe on Thursday you'll be doing something else that takes you near the locksmith. In that case, you'll get the keys duplicated then. If not, it's no crisis, since these are not priority items.

At the end of the week, transfer in green ink every item in this category not completed to next week's notes column. They then take on a kind of priority because, obviously, we don't want to transfer them forever from one week to the next.

You can also upgrade something from green to red ink. If you have put off the letter to Aunt Grace for two weeks, and the week she wants Johnny approacheth, transfer it to the next week in red ink. That means, "do this in your first spare minute."

When you think of a low-priority item, write it immediately on your low-priority list, or write it on the memo pad or notebook and transfer it when convenient to the low-priority list. *Do not carry and transfer things on your day-to-day lists that are not priority items (things you must do that day).* That creates a lot of duplication, which we are trying to avoid. Every day should be as much of a *fait accompli* as possible.

We will deal with even longer-range goals in the last chapter.

Organizing Weekly "No-Choice" Items

There is one other group of activities to consider. This group comprises what usually are weekly activities without a given time frame, things about which you have little choice—you just have to find time for them. This category consists of such things as:

Buying groceries

Doing the laundry

Going to the bank

General apartment cleaning

Try to schedule these things into your calendar because there are optimal times for doing each of them.

For instance, your grocery store, bank and laundry are crowded at certain times and uncrowded at others. If you buy groceries haphazardly or just when you need them, chances are the store will be crowded and shopping will be difficult. But if you set aside a certain time each week when you know the store isn't crowded to do your weekly shopping, it goes more smoothly. (This necessitates some advance meal planning which we will not consider in this book.) Of course there are always incidentals you'll need, but you can pick them up at a smaller grocery store.

The bank is always crowded on Mondays, Fridays and during lunch time. Try to schedule one bank trip per week at an uncrowded time.

The laundry is less crowded in the early evening during the week.

Write these dates in pencil in your datebook and try not to let something else supersede them. Adding them to your datebook helps you stick to your plan.

Week 1 draws to a close. You have learned how to organize your day-by-day activities as well as your lesser priorities so that you have a handle on getting them done.

For now, we are finished with time. As you continue through the next weeks, write in your notebook things about your schedule that bother you. You might find, for instance, that the dance lesson you take every Thursday at 2:00 isn't really at the most convenient time for you. Maybe there is one at a better time you could switch to. In finding and putting your finger on problems, you are more than halfway towards finding the solution and being more organized.

2
WEEK TWO:
ORGANIZING SPACE

In relativistic physics, space and time are different aspects of the same thing—opposite sides of the same coin, if you will.

In organizational physics, we have a similar situation. As you begin to organize your time, you will uncover more time, which you can then use to begin tackling spatial organization problems that you never seemed to have time for before. You can use your datebook (a measurement of time really) to help you. As your space becomes more efficiently organized, you will find still more time which you can use in whatever way you wish. You can play a game of golf. Or keep organizing your time and space until you have uncovered an infinite amount of both, a state otherwise known as nirvana.

Space refers to your apartment or home, your bedroom, your hall closet. Many people who have a problem organizing time may be perfectly organized when it comes to space (and possibly vice versa, though that seems less likely). If that is your case, adjust your week accordingly: you probably could save some time by skipping this chapter altogether!

But, if your hall closet is a mess; if you can't find a needle and thread when you need to sew on a button; if you have knives in the spoon section of your silverware drawer; if some poltergeist seems to move things from where you put them the last time you used them—you probably should give this chapter a chance.

Use this week to carefully consider the following questions.

DISORGANIZED OR JUST LAZY?

No offense, but it's quite possible that your problem in organizing space might stem from sheer laziness rather than lacking a means of organization. For instance, I have a hall closet. With hangers. But when I get home, one of my sweetest pleasures is *not* using it. My coat, hat, scarf, umbrella and gloves end up on the sofa in the living room.

This is laziness more than disorganization. Of course, laziness breeds disorganization. Once your living room starts filling up with coats and clutter, you are earmarked as both a lazy and a disorganized (not to mention a low-down, dirty and otherwise disreputable) person.

The problem with laziness is that there is very little a book can do to cure it (a boot maybe, but not a book). But there are things that can help.

One of the causes of laziness is a feeling of helplessness. When things are in incredible disarray and seem too overwhelming to cope with, the easiest thing to do is not to cope. You let things slide, which, of course, only makes them worse.

Antidotes to Laziness

If you tackle a major chore a little at a time, it doesn't seem so overwhelming.

- *Breaking down.* This does not mean you—it

means turning a large undertaking into several smaller chores. You can begin to chip away at it until it's done. For instance, let's assume your basement is a mess. A basement is a pretty big space to handle, but if you break it down into such chores as

> throw out all old newspapers
> clean the laundry room
> throw out any junk that is no good
> collect all "good" junk for a garage sale

it becomes easier to face. Maybe you do just one chore a week, but you're still getting it done— gradually.

A second method, instead of dividing by chores, is to budget by time. For example: assign an hour a week to the basement and work that amount of time. This way, however, still leaves you the problem of where to start.

In chapter 4, we will discuss how to use your datebook to schedule and get these chores done on a long-term basis.

• *Accepting (to a degree, of course) and working with it.* If you, for instance, know that you will never hang your coat in the hall closet, buy yourself an attractive coat rack. It keeps the coat off the sofa and keeps things fairly organized. Or try hooks by the back door, in your mud room or in a back hall if you live in a house.

• *Hiding it.* I have a friend whose clothes landed wherever he took them off. His wife first threatened divorce before he hit upon a rather ingenious solution. Having a large bedroom, he simply built another wall and made himself a dressing room where he now dresses and undresses. It may be total chaos in there (I'm quite certain his wife never ventures in), but it keeps the bedroom and the rest of the house unlittered. Containing or confining chaos may not be as good as organizing it. But it's better than nothing.

This is an unusual example and may not work for you, but it does, I think, make a good point. Try to be ingenious when you are facing an organization or laziness problem. Be creative. All kinds of possibilities will open up to you.

For example:
You can never find your keys when you're ready to leave the house.

Put a small dish or hook by the front door where you immediately put your keys when you come in and pick them up when you leave.

You get a lot of mail—and a lot of junk mail—that you don't get a chance to sort through every day, so it winds up cluttering up a table or desk.

Create in/out boxes for mail that has and hasn't been dealt with. Use ordinary shoe or other boxes. At least it will keep your mail orderly until you get around to it, which you do at least once a week.

Toys all over the house?

The proverbial toy box is a lifesaver, if you can refrain from throwing the kids in it when things get really bad! One family has a toy box on wheels so that Mom can simply pull it around the house, tossing in toys as she goes.

Change, wallet, rings, loose scraps of paper, and

so forth end up on top of your dresser when you get home.

Get a dresser organizer with a place for these items to be held neatly.

You've got menus from a pizza place, a Chinese restaurant and other carry-out food services cluttering up your kitchen counter.

Thumbtack them to the inside of a kitchen cupboard (or use magnets, on metal cabinets), where they will be out of the way but accessible when you need them.

You can also do this with business cards from plumbers, electricians, locksmiths, and other specialists.

Your family observes the anti-litter laws—except inside the car.

Get a "car caddy" with a place for litter as well as space for change for tolls, a box of tissues, cups and other things that tend to get tossed around the inside of a car.

Your closet is a mess and you can never find the right hanger when you need it.

With apologies to Christina Crawford, give all your wire hangers back to the dry cleaner and buy a bunch of nice wood or plastic ones. Ones that will do for both shirts and pants.

You've collected newspaper clippings, post cards, snapshots, recipes—where do you put them so they don't get lost or soiled?

Get a bulletin board. You'll be surprised at how fast it fills up (which also means you'll have to weed it every so often).

Your tools are all tangled up and mixed together in a tool box or drawer.

Put up a pegboard in the garage, basement or even a back hallway. It's simply the best method for keeping tools in plain sight as well as orderly.

DISORGANIZED OR JUST LACKING SPACE?

One of the most difficult things to cope with when you are trying to get organized is a lack of space. It's hard to make things look neat when the closet is overflowing into the hallway; when the medicine cabinet won't hold all your prescriptions and cosmetics and toothpaste; when your kitchen is only slightly larger than a stockpot.

You have my sympathy. I lived in a studio apartment once.

But ignoring these things won't make them better. The clutter won't go away (as a matter of fact, clutter seems to be slightly more reproductive than rabbits). Take heart. If this is your problem, there are things that can be done.

Rule #1. Throw things away. You of all people cannot afford to be a pack rat. When you finish a newspaper or a magazine, throw it away. Go through your closets and throw out other thing. you never, never use.

Rule #2. Give things away. It may be hard to throw away certain things, even though you know you'll never use them again. So give it to a friend.

Go through your closets and drawers and select the things that are too good to simply throw away and give them to someone who will use them. You can always borrow them back later—and when was the last time you used that carving set, anyway?

Rule #3. Store things. "Sure, where?" you ask. And I'm glad you did.

If you live in a house, you probably are not having this problem. Of course, if you are, the basement is an obvious solution (neatly, though, neatly).

If you live in an apartment building, talk to your superintendent. Most buildings have storage space for tenants where they can put things that they don't use or need too often. You will probably want to store such things as

> luggage
> Christmas decorations
> camping gear
> tools
> winter coats in the summer time

Make sure everything you store is carefully boxed and labeled with your name; keep a list of things you have stored.

Commercial storage space is available in most cities. And if you don't need too much space, you'll be surprised how reasonable it is. Often these places offer twenty-four-hour access. Since this is not the most convenient form of storage, put away only those items you don't use more than three or four times a year.

Rule #4. Be inventive. A bicycle standing in the hallway is in the way. Hanging on the wall, it can be an interesting piece of art.

Here are some other ideas:

IN THE BATHROOM

Buy a little shelf. Take all your attractive bottles of cologne out of the medicine cabinet and display them on this shelf. You can even decant such things as mouthwash and put them out, too.

If it's not already so, *enclose the lower part of your sink with a cabinet.* It'll look better and give you lots of new storage space.

Keep cleaning supplies in a plastic bucket and store inside the shower. Obviously you will have to move them when you shower, but it will keep them out of the way the rest of the day.

IN THE BEDROOM

Build a platform bed with drawers underneath for loads of storage space.

Use sweater boxes to store under a regular frame bed.

Hang a shoe rack on the inside of your closet door.

Build an extra level of shelves in the top part of your closet for items you don't need very often.

Store your seasonal clothes somewhere else in the off-season, so you'll have more closet space.

A woman in the clothing business simply built a high-tech metal rack across one wall of her bedroom. She has lots of bright and colorful outfits, which she hangs very neatly on this rack instead of in a closet. The effect is a personal statement that is fun and also attractive.

IN THE KITCHEN

Julia Child, who is not a good friend of mine—though I really wish she were—can be your example. Hang your cooking implements. Her pots, pans, whisks, spoons and knives hang in open sight around her kitchen. There are many ways to do this, from racks to peg boards to hooks in the ceiling or wall.

Store foodstuff in canisters and jars out on the counter, if there's not room inside cupboards.

Buy racks for appliance accessories. Often appliances that have accompanying accessories, such as food processors, offer racks to hold these accessories. They are generally inexpensive and worth the price.

IN THE LIVING ROOM

Build shelves.

Build more shelves.

Build shelves with cabinets underneath for hiding things away.

If you're really desperate, you even can keep flat items like brooms and ironing boards behind the sofa or the draperies. (If you're really desperate.)

DISORGANIZED WITH NO EXCUSES?

If you're not simply lazy, and you do have plenty of room, the fact of the matter may just be that you lack a good spatial organization scheme. And that, lucky for you, is the easiest problem to solve.

To begin, spend a day observing your spatial organization problems. From the time you get up in the morning until just before you go to bed at night, be keenly aware of your space problems. Look for things even if they are not part of that day's agenda to compile as comprehensive a list as possible. Have your notebook by your side to write down things that bother you even if you're not sure it's related to spatial organization. (Use a different page from the one on which during the day you write the things to do or buy.)

A sample day:

1. In the morning there wasn't enough soap, so I had to go get it in the kitchen.*

2. The medicine cabinet is dirty and a mess.*

3. I couldn't find the blue sweater I wanted (closet a mess).*

4. Ran out of corn flakes.

5. Car keys. Where?*

6. Late for dance lesson.

7. Can't stand moving the vacuum cleaner every time I want to get out the card table.*

8. Had to retrieve two spoons from dishwasher and wash before dinner.*

9. And, yes, the basement is an abomination.*

After you have spent a day compiling this list, take some time to go over it. Mark which items truly are and which are not spatial organization problems. On this list, they are designated with an asterisk; for example, item number one. It's no fun to have to go looking for soap in the morning, especially if you're wet. Simply move an extra bar soap to a convenient spot closer to the shower.

Item number four may or may not be a spatial organization problem. We shall consider how to deal with running out of things in chapter 4.

Now that you've gone through the entire list and marked which organizational problems relate to space, let's consider how to deal with them.

Compartmentalization

Just as the brain has different sections for dealing with speech and sight and memory, so should your space be compartmentalized. Keep bath items in the bathroom, kitchen items in the kitchen. Your linen closet should be devoted to linen, your clothes closet to clothes. If this seems obvious, take a look and make sure you are not breaking this rule, even if only in minor ways. That's right, I'm talking about your top dresser drawer, too.

It's easier to keep track of things and find things when they are kept in one place, and even more so if it's a logical place. This may require some rearranging of closets, drawers and shelves, but I think you'll find it's worth it.

Even if you do manage to have things in some kind of basic order, you might find things spilling over onto each other so that you still have to look when you want something. If this is the case, compartmentalize a little further.

If you keep all your nuts, bolts, screws and nails in a coffee can all mixed together, think about this: How about putting all these various items in a plastic box with twenty different subcompartments, the kind fishermen use for tackle? When you need something, you don't have to dig around for it. Just open the lid, and there it is. And when you run out of something, you know it, which you never do when things are all jumbled together.

Most people keep their silverware in a similar arrangement. But you can push this way beyond silverware and nails. Install dividers in your drawers and extra shelves wherever they fit and seem logical. For instance, if you stack your sweaters five or six high in a closet and topple the pile whenever you want the sweater on the bottom, add shelves that allow only two sweaters to be stacked.

This week, you have concentrated on uncovering the exact nature of your space problems. Implement immediately any quick solutions you have found. If a shoe rack will help your closet immensely, put it on your list of things to buy this week and get it.

In week 4 (chapter 4) we will deal with solving

the more major space problems. In the meantime, continue observing and adding onto the list of space (as well as other organization) problems that you started earlier.

3

WEEK THREE:
ORGANIZING MONEY
THINGS & THOUGHTS

No doubt as you begin to organize your closets, you will uncover a few skeletons. That's because organization breeds organization. As you begin to organize the rest of your life, anything that's not organized will stick out like a sore thumb.

In week 3, you will start on clearing up some odds and ends that plague you.

ORGANIZING MONEY

Your problem with money may be like some people's problems with space: You don't have enough of it. Just as they have to learn to live within their four walls, you have to live within your four—or five—figures (anybody making six figures should be paying someone else to organize their money).

If you are in over your head financially, you need more help than this book can give you. But if dealing with money fits more in the category of a tremendous hassle, this book can help.

Make a Budget

The first thing you have to do if you can't seem to stretch your funds from paycheck to paycheck is make a budget. (Again, there are whole books devoted to financial planning that go into much more detail than we can. The idea here is to give you a basic plan to get you started.)

It is best to prepare a budget on a monthly basis, since most regular bills are monthly. (When figuring out your monthly expenses, multiply any weekly bills times four.)

- *Add up all your fixed monthly expenditures.*
Fixed expenditures are those things that stay the
same every month, such as your rent, loan pay-
ments, insurance premiums, and so forth. It also
includes such expenses as your phone and electric
bills, even though they vary from month to month.
Just take an average of the past few months' bills.
(Part of your phone bill—your long distance calls,
requests for information—can be controlled, so
you may want to eliminate them from your esti-
mate and take only the part of your phone bill that
remains the same each month.)

- *Add up your monthly income and subtract the
monthly expenditures.* (If the latter is larger than
the former, you are in trouble.)

The remainder is the money you have left
each month to use on variable expenses such as
food, clothing, entertainment, and others. While
these things may be necessities, you have more
control over them than you do over your fixed
expenses. You can buy hamburger instead of
steak.

Let's say the amount of money you have left
over is $600. How do you want to budget this
money to get you through the month? Food is your
most basic expense—could you eat on $50 a week?
No? How about $75? Possibly.

Then budget $75 a week for food. You now
have $300 left.

Clothing is a necessity but not one you need to
renew every month. Earmark $100 a month for
clothing. What you don't spend, add to next
month's allotment; let it build up so when you need
it, you have it.

There is now only $200 left for entertainment and other miscellaneous expenses. Not much, but then you *are* on a budget. Some of this you might want to save for the proverbial rainy day. Put away $40 a month; this leaves you with $160 for your other expenses, or $40 a week. Watch this $40 very carefully. Try not to go over it; if you do, make it up the next week by spending only $30. If you are consistently spending more than $40 a week, you will need to rethink your budget.

Obviously, the amounts in each category will vary with your particular finances. The point is to get you thinking in terms of *taking control of your money*.

ORGANIZING BILLS

Pay your bills once a month.

As bills come in, put them in a special place in your desk. Here also put solicitations for charities or causes that you feel inclined to support. Once a month, sit down with your checkbook and pay them all. In this way, you never have to wonder whether a bill has been paid or not. If you got the bill, it got paid. Any bills that come in after this date get paid next month.

Paying bills like this helps to keep your checkbook orderly, too, because at the same time you pay your bills, also balance your account against your monthly bank statement and check off last month's canceled checks.

For those few checks that you write during

the month for groceries or gas or whatever, make a quick notation in your checkbook noting the details (amount, payee). Do the arithmetic on "money night." If you write a lot of other checks, this might not work for you. In that case, keep track of the math as you write the checks.

ORGANIZING THINGS

Things is a disorganized word. It doesn't really mean anything. It's vague.

Yet there are a lot of *things* that we have not addressed so far that still need organization, like books and records and magazines. Maybe you have a drawer full of loose photographs or newspaper clippings you want to save. Although you have your own things that need organization, we'll use these as examples.

Records

Records are a good place to begin. If you have quite a few albums mixed together, the first level of organization is to separate the various categories of music (folk, rock, jazz, classical), and so forth. If your collection requires it, the next step is to arrange the albums alphabetically by composer or artist (but still within their separate categories). Elvis Presley gets filed under the P's in the rock group, the Beatles under the B's.

This system isn't foolproof. Here are some tricky recordings. How would you file them?

FOR THE RECORD

Album	Where to File
1. Puccini, *Madama Butterfly,* sung by Leontyne Price, *et al.*	Under Puccini, classical. Or: Puccini, opera, classical.
2. Neil Diamond and Barbra Streisand, *You Don't Send Me Flowers*	File under your favorite, or file alphabetically. Rock.
3. Caballé sings Rossini Rarities	A toughie. Rossini, classical.
4. Coltrane and Ellington	Same rationale as #2. Jazz.
5. Ella sings Gershwin	Fitzgerald, jazz, even though it contradicts the precedent set by #3. (In classical music, as in #3, the composer seems more important than the artist; this is purely a personal prejudice.)

6. Miles Davis plays *Porgy & Bess*	Davis, jazz; same reasoning as #5.
7. Boulez conducts Wagner	Wagner, classical.
8. Baroque Favorites (with selections from Handel, Bach, Pachelbel and Vivaldi)	I bought this record for Pachelbel's *Canon*, so I have filed it under the *P*'s, classical.
9. Joan Baez sings Bob Dylan	Baez, rock.
10. Andy Williams, *Somewhere My Love*	Throw out.

You can see from this that every scheme of organization has its flaws; however, you can minimize them by being consistent. If you know you tend to file an album under the name of the person who sings it rather than under the composer of the music, you will know where to look for it.

Books

The same rule applies to books when you start to organize them. Be consistent.

If a quick perusal of your shelves will uncover what you are looking for, you may not feel the need to organize your books at all. Other people organize their books by height, attractiveness, or binding. But someone with a large library might want to consider the following plan:

Separate fiction books from nonfiction. Arrange fiction titles alphabetically by author, nonfiction by subject matter. (For example: Put all history books together. If you have a lot of history books, keep Civil War, World War I and World War II books in their own clusters within the history category.) You may need a third category—reference books, for your dictionary, thesaurus, books of quotations and encyclopedia.

This generally is sufficient for most people. However, if your library is very important to you and you use it quite often, you might want to make your own card catalogue. Use 3 x 5 cards, which you can keep in a recipe box. List every book by three different categories on three separate cards—by title (eliminating the articles *a*, *an* and *the*), by author (forget your reference books here; Webster didn't really write your dictionary), and by subject matter (usually this category is omitted for fiction, but sometimes fiction has a broad category, such as "war" or "love" or "the South" you might want to consider). On each card, make a brief note of where the book can be found. Alphabetize the cards within the three categories in your file box, and you have a system as good as any library's, though maybe a touch simpler.

Magazines

You may see little value in saving magazines. Consider this: Old copies of *Life* can go for upwards of $10 in some bookshops.

Many people do like to keep their old magazines, especially ones like *Gourmet*, *National Geographic* and *Architectural Digest*.

The solution to organizing magazines is an easy one. Most magazine publishers offer reasonably priced, attractive, hardcover binders that will conveniently hold a year's worth of magazines. This enables you to store your magazines standing up in a neat, orderly way on your bookshelf. As an added service, many magazines also sell, or give away, yearly indices of the magazine's contents. When you want to refer to an article in an old issue, it's easy to locate.

If you save magazines that don't have their own binders for sale, you could always buy the *Gourmet* binders, for instance, relabel them and put your old *Newsweeks* inside. Make sure first that the magazines are of the same size and format.

Other Things

Earlier we mentioned loose photographs as something that might need organization. Obviously, these just need to be put into photo albums. If you take a lot of pictures, however, you might want to put together albums devoted to specific vacations or occasions, such as "Europe 1980," "Caribbean Cruise," and "High School Reunion." Then you can look at the pictures you want to look at without having to wade through a lot of others.

There are undoubtedly hundreds of other things in your life that don't seem to have a neat little nook and cranny they can fit into. There are two ways to handle them, whatever they are.

FILE THEM

Perhaps the biggest helper for organizing loose bits of information in your life is a filing cabinet. Not many people have them in their homes because filing cabinets seem too office-like. And that's too bad, because they can be wonders of organization as well as attractive. You don't have to get gray or army green; as a matter of fact, offices rarely use those dinosaurs anymore. Filing cabinets now come in a variety of shapes and colors. There are even some you could put right in your living room, place your TV set or a vase on top of it, and nobody would guess that it was a filing cabinet.

Use your filing cabinet to keep all your paperwork organized. File away all your old bills, each in their own alphabetized folder. Keep receipts for things you buy, so if something needs to be returned, you'll have the receipt handy. File warranties and instruction manuals for appliances.

If you tear items out of magazines and newspapers, a filing system will keep these clippings from becoming lost forever. For example: If you read about a good restaurant you'd like to try, clip the article or review and place it in a folder marked *Restaurants*.

BOX THEM

Get some boxes, put in your "things," label the boxes clearly on the outside and stash them away—probably never to be seen again. For instance, I have a shoebox filled with roadmaps, tucked away in a closet. If I ever plan to drive through Montana again, I'll know just where to look for a hopelessly outdated map that's guaranteed to get me lost. Nonetheless, I know it's there.

Organizing Your Thoughts

If *things* is a nebulous word, *thoughts* is perhaps even more so. There are so many possibilities when considering organizing thoughts. Giving two examples will help you adapt organizational strategies to your own situation.

PLANNING A SPEECH OR REPORT

You have to give a speech or write a report. Maybe a club you belong to needs to launch a fund-raising drive, and you're the chairperson of the committee. Here's what you do:

• *Sit down and collect or organize your thoughts.* What are the things you should talk or write about? Make a list.

For instance, you might write down:

I.   *Current state of club finances.*
II.   *What we want this money for.*
III. *Fund-raising drives we've had in the past.*
IV.   *Possibilities for this one.*
V.   *How much money we need to raise.*

This then becomes your general outline.

• *Refine your thinking.* As you begin to do research, place the information you collect under these various categories. (Of course, you can also expand the number of categories if more occur to you later.) For instance, point II might develop to look something like this:

II. What we want this money for.

    A. *Our adopted child in Burma.*
        1. His food expenses.
        2. Schooling.
        3. Clothing.
    B. *New hospital wing - we pledged $1000.*
    C. *Member John Doe died, and his family needs assistance.*

    List the general heading at the top of a 3 x 5 card and place each item on a separate card. You can shift the cards around and group related information together.

    You can be lazier and take notes on sheets of

legal paper, especially if it is a short paper or speech that doesn't require much research. Make a notation in the margin as to what category that item will fall under. For instance, if you are combing through the club's minutes researching past years' fund-raising drives, you might make notes that look like this:

1978 Paper drive made $650
*1979 Rented civic auditorium for a dance-
    lost $190*

In the margin, you would write a Roman numeral III to indicate that this information pertains to that part of the outline. When you compose the final report or speech, cross these items off as you use them.

PLANNING A PARTY

The second example deals with planning an event. This time you are going to have a party. After you've decided what kind of a party it will be, you

• *Sit down and make a list.* Write down the components that will make your party successful. This process is almost the same as coming up with points for an outline. For instance, you probably would write down:

Food

Drinks

Music

Then, of course, you need to break each of these down into specifics. The category *Drinks* would spawn a list like this:

Bourbon

Vodka

Gin

Wine

Beer

Mixers - club soda, tonic water,
orange juice

Coke

7-Up

Ice

As you shop for your party and pick up these items, cross them off your list.

You can see how every large project or event is comprised of many components. Each whole can be broken down into smaller parts that are easier to handle. When you grasp the knack of dividing and conquering, you're on your way to being organized.

A brief mention of the new technology: Home computers, for instance, which are taking the country by storm, can be extremely useful organizational tools. They can help you with your finances and store amazing amounts of material on tiny floppy disks. A computer is a rather specialized item. If you are contemplating purchasing one, the manufacturers and stores that sell them will be more than happy to demonstrate how a computer can help you in many different areas.

4
WEEK FOUR: PULLING IT ALL TOGETHER

After three weeks of organizing everything from the time you go shopping to the way you think, you may wonder what you need a week 4 for.

Well, first of all, it would be very disorderly not to tie up the few loose threads we left dangling throughout this book. And secondly, it is important to realize that in "real life" you won't always spend a week working on organizing time, then on space, then on things. You have to control, to organize, all these things simultaneously.

THE MASTER PLAN

Here we integrate all the elements into a plan that can work all the time.

Throughout the past three weeks, you have been writing down things that bother you in your notebook (keeping them separate from the daily memos you make that go immediately into your datebook or onto your shopping or errand list). You have also noted some projects, such as arranging your books and records, that you may want to do but didn't have time for immediately. Take a few minutes and glance through the notebook, adding such long-range items to the list you've been compiling.

Undoubtedly, there are things on the list that bother you that we can do nothing about here—the fact that your spouse squeezes the toothpaste tube in the middle (an organized person would never do that, right?). Eliminate them—not your spouse, just that item—from the list. Restrict the list to only those things that relate directly to organization, whether it be a time, spatial or other organizational problem.

Perhaps you are left with a list like this:

Dance lesson is at inconvenient time
Basement a mess
Hall closet a mess
Ran out of cornflakes
Would like to organize my records
Get some shelves built for the living room
Need to buy a filing cabinet

Here's how to handle it:

• *Consider which items are small chores, things that can be taken care of immediately.* Rescheduling your dance lesson is certainly one of these. You might make a little pencil note in your datebook to talk to your instructor about this the next time you have a lesson (then cross it off this list).

Buying a filing cabinet is also something that can be done fairly easily. This you will want to put on your weekly list of things to do; it is something not planned for any given day, rather something you will do this week when you get around to it. (Again, once you have put it on your weekly list, cross it off this one.)

• *Consider which items are very time-consuming to handle.* The items "basement a mess," "hall closet a mess," "would like to organize my records" and "get some shelves built for the living room" are probably jobs that will take a good deal of time. Perhaps your next few weeks are fairly busy and you know you won't have time to do them; it would be pointless to put them on a weekly list.

• *Keep track of long-range items in a separate area of your datebook.* (You can keep this list somewhere else—it really doesn't matter. But having as many things as you can organized in your datebook gives you just one source to refer to.) These are the long-range goals we've mentioned several times throughout this book—goals too monumental to tackle all at once or immediately, but things you don't want to lose track of, either.

• *Work on long-range items one at a time or a little at a time.* For instance, arranging your records may be something that will only take an hour or so. When a lean week comes along, move this chore onto your weekly list and do it that week (crossing it off your long-range list then, of course). On the other hand, if you have hundreds of records you may want to plan on arranging just your jazz albums one week and other categories in subsequent weeks.

Do the same thing with the basement and hall closet. Break them down into smaller projects if necessary, and schedule these small projects onto your weekly lists a little at a time.

• *Refer back often to this long-range list.* Don't forget about it.

To recap, you will have three different scheduling lists for organizing your activities:

Daily

Weekly

Long-range

When something new comes up, place it on any one of the three, depending upon what it is. Something that gets placed on the long-range list, however, will gradually work its way to the weekly and ultimately the daily list. If you see something on the long-range list and simply do it when you have the spare time, do not transfer it to the next list. It got done (your goal); just cross it off.

THE SHOPPING SPREE

You may have noticed that I did not cover the item "ran out of corn flakes." (And I'm much too organized just to overlook something like that, right?)

Of course you want to put corn flakes on your shopping list to purchase the next time you are in the store. But is there a way of getting so organized that you can avoid running out of things in the first place?

Organization means never having to be caught off guard. (*Never* might be too strong a word, but the intention is correct.) One of life's curses is to have to run out and get something when you need it—especially when you could have had it on hand.

The way to avoid it is fairly simple, though it takes a little effort in the beginning. Once you've got the system in place, it is self-perpetuating. (If you have a severe space problem, you may have to pare down this system accordingly, but it will still work fairly well with some modification.)

Here's what to do.

- *Take an inventory*. This won't work if your

shelves and cupboards are a mess, so get them fairly well in order. You are compiling a list of your supplies and provisions. Write down everything you have on hand that it would be really wonderful not ever to run out of again.

Start with the kitchen cupboard where you keep canned goods and other nonperishables. Record items like:

Tomato paste

Spaghetti noodles

Beef broth

Soup

Ketchup

Flour

Sugar

Salt

You get the idea. Next, look underneath the kitchen sink and write down:

Cleanser

Soap pads

Window cleaner

Dish detergent

Sponges

Moving right along, take a trip into your bathroom and check out your bath supplies:

Soap

Shampoo

Toothpaste

Deodorant

Bowl cleaner

Razor blades

Cosmetics

Check out any other areas where you keep supplies: laundry room, liquor cabinet, basement, pantry. Don't forget to list such items as:

Light bulbs

Fuses

Candles

Detergent

Bleach

Sodas and mixers

• *Go on a shopping trip and buy extras of these items to keep on hand.* In some cases, space may not permit you to have extras (we will deal with this in a minute). Of some things, like shampoo, you may only need one extra bottle, whereas things that get used up faster (perhaps vodka?) will require several.

You can buy extras of perishable items like butter and keep them in your freezer, or an extra half-gallon of milk if you know you will use it before it spoils (actually, you can freeze milk, too). There are also lots of foods that don't need refrigeration until they are opened—mayonnaise, mustard, jams and jellies, olives, to name a few.

The purpose of this shopping trip is not to make your home look like a supermarket, however, so use a little common sense. If there are things that you don't mind running out of, omit them. But do buy the things you use a lot and especially those things that are really aggravating to run out of. (I hate, for instance, to have to wash my hair with bar soap, but I had to many times before I kept extra shampoo on hand.)

• *Stash your goods neatly in your cupboards and on your shelves.* If you thought space was going to be a problem, you might be surprised by how little extra space you really need. Extra boxes and cans of things stack very neatly on top of and behind one another.

• *Write down an item on your shopping list every time you use up the next-to-the-last one.* When you open the last bottle of shampoo, write *shampoo* on your list so you have a new bottle by the time you need it. (With items like bar soap, you may want to keep several as a buffer against running out, in which case put *soap* on your list when you get down to two or three bars.)

For people who really don't have the room to implement this kind of system, as well as for those items you use very slowly, you can accomplish the same result by waiting until your bottle of shampoo, or ketchup, or bourbon is one half to three quarters empty before writing it down on your list. But *don't wait for things to be gone or nearly gone.* This way you should have a replacement by the time you run out.

After your system is set up, that's all you have to do to keep it going. No system is foolproof. You still are going to run out of things, but it will happen a lot less often, and there will be a lot less aggravation in your life.

A Word About
Disorganization . . .

Don't get too carried away by your zeal. Pause to consider that we are not ants. Or androids.

While organization does help us to run our lives more smoothly, we don't want to push it *too* far. You probably know people who do, and let's face it, they are not always the most pleasant to be around. (We are safe to disparage them here, as it's highly unlikely they will be reading a book on how to get organized.) Their lives have a mission. They do nothing unless according to plan. They have a place for everything, and everything is in its place.

Being organized is psychologically rewarding in and of itself. There is a part of us that loves system and pattern and logic. It's possible to see how getting organized could become addictive. (Let's face it. Probably none of us will have this problem.)

But there is another side to our brains (psychologists say that it is the right half) that gravitates towards the random, the unstructured, the disorderly. Just as we can love the geometric repeats and patterns of an artist like M.C. Escher, we can also enjoy the seemingly haphazard, chaotic canvases of Jackson Pollock.

Obviously, some of us lean more towards one than the other. But you should look at your system of organization as a means to helping you enjoy more fully your time off, your sloppy times. After you've done your chores and accomplished what you had hoped to accomplish in a given day, relax.

For example, wanting an ice cream cone is not the kind of activity one puts down on one's list. If you want an ice cream cone, you want it now, not at 3:45 after you've picked up Johnny at school and before you go to the dry cleaner. So go ahead, go out and get one now (unless, of course, you're dieting) even at the expense of being impulsive, and even if you go right by the ice cream store on the way to pick up Johnny.

We can never become totally organized; there are parts of us and things in our lives that will defy totally any attempt to classify, rearrange or otherwise organize. Give into them and enjoy them—revel in both sides of yourself.

About the Author

Gary Holland lives in the most chaotic city in the world (well, he's never been to Tokyo, which he hears might rival New York), and he is organized enough to hold down a regular job and do considerable writing on the side, as well as to cook, clean, do his own laundry and otherwise maintain an apartment without the help of a housekeeper.